household

WISDOM

Tessa Evelegh

household
WISDOM

Traditional housekeeping for the contemporary home

LORENZ BOOKS

This edition is published by Lorenz Books, an imprint of Anness Publishing Ltd, Hermes House, 88–89 Blackfriars Road, London SE1 8HA; tel. 020 7401 2077; fax 020 7633 9499

www.lorenzbooks.com; www.annesspublishing.com

If you like the images in this book and would like to investigate using them for publishing, promotions or advertising, please visit our website www.practicalpictures.com for more information.

UK agent: The Manning Partnership Ltd; tel. 01225 478444; fax 01225 478440; sales@manning-partnership.co.uk

UK distributor: Grantham Book Services Ltd; tel. 01476 541080; fax 01476 541061; orders@gbs.tbs-ltd.co.uk

North American agent/distributor: National Book Network; tel. 301 459 3366; fax 301 429 5746; www.nbnbooks.com

Australian agent/distributor: Pan Macmillan Australia; tel. 1300 135 113; fax 1300 135 103; customer.service@macmillan.com.au

New Zealand agent/distributor: David Bateman Ltd; tel. (09) 415 7664; fax (09) 415 8892

PUBLISHER: Joanna Lorenz
MANAGING EDITOR: Helen Sudell
PROJECT EDITOR: Simona Hill
DESIGNER: Louise Clements
EDITORIAL READER: Penelope Goodare
PRODUCTION CONTROLLER: Darren Price

ETHICAL TRADING POLICY
Because of our ongoing ecological investment programme, you, as our customer, can have the pleasure and reassurance of knowing that a tree is being cultivated on your behalf to naturally replace the materials used to make the book you are holding. For further information about this scheme, go to www.annesspublishing.com/trees

A CIP catalogue record for this book is available from the British Library.

Disclaimer

The recipes in this book have all been tried and tested, but any plant, cosmetic or animal substance can cause allergic reactions in certain people. Neither the author nor the publishers can be held responsible for inappropriate use of any of the remedies or beauty treatments, nor for excessive intake or mistaken identity of any of the plants.

Contents

Introduction   6

On the Table   8
   Elegant Table Linen   12
   China & Porcelain   14
   Sparkling Glasses   16
   Touching Wood   18
   Cutlery & Candelabra   20

The Linen Press   22
   Perfumed Closets   26
   Laundering Lore   28
   New Life for Linen & Lace   30
   A Stitch in Time   32
   Scenting the Room   34

Body & Soul   36
   Pampering Treats   40
   Bathtime Fragrances   42
   Skin Care   44
   Healing Treatments   46
   Medicinal Remedies   48

Treats in Store   50
   Flavoured Oils & Vinegars   54
   Preserved Fruits   56
   Chutneys, Pickles & Mustard 58
   Jams & Jellies   60
   Teas, Tisanes & Herbal Drinks 62

Index   64

Introduction

Fast-track living in the 21st century leaves us with little time to appreciate what it really takes to make a home. In the desperate race to get everything done, we may overlook the importance of nurturing our homes on a day-to-day basis. And in our throwaway society, many traditional homemaker's tricks have been abandoned in favour of convenience. Yet, increasingly, it seems, we are beginning to yearn for simpler times, when furniture and household items were made to last, and when housekeepers were proud of skills that had been passed down through the generations and were more to do with preservation and self-sufficiency than replacement.

Developed over centuries, when every household aimed at a self-sufficiency unheard of today, traditional household skills necessarily encompassed a wide range of domestic activity. Homemakers of the past kept house on a daily basis, keeping the house clean and well presented with household linen and clothing regularly laundered and sweet smelling. Working on a budget, they knew how to extend the life of fabrics, and how to transform garden produce and other ingredients into a variety of flavourings and long-lasting foods, including bottled fruits, jams, jellies, chutneys and pickles. They

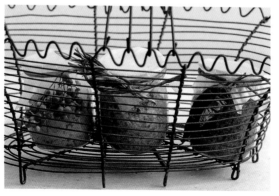

Delicious home-made mustards make a wonderful gift, especially when attractively decorated and presented in a set.

could produce a formidable range of simple but effective skin-cleansing and beauty treatments that were free of the harsh chemicals and preservatives that are ever-present in contemporary cosmetics. Not able to afford the expense of a doctor's visit, or perhaps being too far away from one, they also had to be able to treat a host of minor ailments from chapped lips and bruises to colds, coughs and sore throats. They also knew the secrets of concocting reviving herbal teas and tonics from home-grown or gathered ingredients.

We can learn an incredible amount from the practices of bygone days, but however nostalgic we may feel, we also understand that not everything was rosy and there were many practices we have no desire to emulate. For example, using large quantities of bleach in order to whiten linens, as our grandmothers would have done, holds no magic for us. We are also reluctant to give up modern standards of perfection and our requirement for rapid results. So this book has set out to select only those housekeeping skills of yesteryear that we can take full advantage of and that, combined with the best that technology can offer, will contribute much to the smooth and efficient running of a contemporary family household.

In choosing which traditional techniques to include, the aim
has been to concentrate on those that have the closest affinity to
contemporary lifestyles and values. Labour-intensive techniques
have therefore been omitted: cold-water starching, for example, is
no longer necessary for today's easy-care household linens, and
few of us would consider it a desirable or productive use of our
valuable time. The hints and tricks that have been selected are
speedy and often magically effective. There's something
incredible, for example, about rubbing a white heat mark on
antique wooden furniture with a nut and watching the mark
literally disappear before your eyes. It takes very little time, and it
works, because the nut oils replace the oils taken out of the wood
by the heat. A modern chemical product might disguise such a
mark, but it would never be as effective as the traditional remedy,
because the new stain it created would not necessarily match the
colour of the wood being treated.

Some of the simple beauty aids are wonderfully hedonistic in
nature and include soothing body lotions and self-indulgent
scented bath oils and foams. And the careful resource
management of yesteryear produced an amazing variety of
culinary treats. Flavoured oils and vinegars are now being
rediscovered – and when you make your own, you are virtually
unlimited in your choice. The same goes for luxurious items such
as brandied fruits, real marmalade and rosehip jelly; once you've
mastered the basic recipes included here, you can go on to
experiment and produce your own combinations.

However much our current lifestyle may differ from that of
our grandparent's generation, their philosophy for living and using
resources wisely is as relevant today as it always was.

A jug and bowl (top), once essential for washing, have become
romantic reminders of a bygone era.
Even the simplest of posies (right) will bring colour and scent to
your kitchen.

On the Table

Crisp white table linens, sparkling elegant glass,

polished wood, sharp and decorative

cutlery, and a fine china dinner service:

these are the ingredients for a well-

dressed table. Look after them and

they'll serve you well for years to come.

An exquisite dining room, set for a banquet, was the English butler's pride and joy. The solid oak table, polished until it reflected his face; mirror-shiny silver cutlery; sparkling glass and the crispest of white linen were all evidence of a well-run household. In order to achieve a dining room like this, the staff had to learn how to launder household linens, to polish glass to a smear-free sparkle and to clean cutlery while ensuring handles didn't work loose from blades. They were also good at dealing with accidental damage to the table's surface, and spills and stains on the table linen.

Their 'secrets' were second-nature routine habits passed down over the years, and they weren't all necessarily time-consuming. Often forgotten, many are still relevant today and waiting to be rediscovered. For example, although many of us rely on our trusty dishwashers to clean everyday tableware, we may still wash our best china and glassware by hand. Fine glass is too delicate for

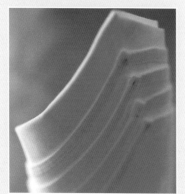

Neatly folded napkins look pleasing on a formally set dining table.

machines and liable to crack in high temperatures. Also, hotter cycles and strong detergents can wash off gold or coloured detail. However, achieving a clear sparkle on hand-washed glass can be much more difficult than in the dishwasher. But if you follow the butler's traditional solution of adding some vinegar to the rinsing water, you'll get a perfect result.

Glassware is not the only feature of our dining areas that can benefit from some knowledge of the many simple tricks of former times. Stains need not permanently spoil tablecloths and napkins if they are dealt with in good time and with the right treatment for the particular food or drink. We can also find out how to make the best use of antique fabrics, which modern technology is so unkind to, and how to look after beautiful wooden furniture with the minimum of fuss.

Sprays of berries are a charming addition to vases of fresh flowers.

Blue and white lend a traditional country look to the table.

For informal dining, modern crockery is available that can easily be washed in a dishwasher but is charmingly rustic in style, especially when teamed with simple cotton table linen.

Diligent housekeepers of the past were also expert at preserving and recycling. We can borrow a few of the techniques they used for smartening worn and fraying edges, but instead of making-do and mending, we can adapt them to suit our modern needs. Adding borders and trims to inexpensive linens, for instance, will give them a fresh fashion look to suit a new season, rather than simply extending their life. We can also share tips on prolonging the life of household furniture and accessories without turning maintenance into a time-consuming chore. For example, drinks coasters were always placed on polished furniture to protect its surface from liquid spills. Green baize cutlery rolls cosseted the best silverware, such as fish knives and forks or special coffee spoons. Cutlery was plunged into jars of warm soapy water after every course, to eliminate chemical damage to the surface caused by food and to avoid wearing away the plating.

Even if you don't own silver cutlery or polished wood furniture, the principles of regular housekeeping habits are handy today: any practice that cuts down on damage or soiling in the first place, greatly eases the housework load, giving you time to enjoy more creative elements of home-making.

Elegant Table Linen

There's something very pleasing about freshly laundered tablecloths and napkins laid out on the table ready for a special meal, or even for more humble daily fare. Dealing with spills immediately will mean less washing later on.

ALTHOUGH WE ARE no longer bound by some of the more fastidious aspects of old-fashioned table etiquette, one enduring requirement is scrupulously clean table linen. To make washing easier, spills and dropped food should be mopped up as soon as possible. Most everyday dining stains can be treated with simple time-honoured treatments, although for dried-in or stubborn stains, modern biological detergents may be appropriate.

Napkins can have a great impact on a table setting. All you need to create an individual look is a 50cm/20in square of fabric, plus some trimmings. You can even make 'antique' napkins by seeking out beautiful old textiles, such as linen, and simply cutting away any worn or torn parts. Napkins can also be personalized with a little embroidery or trimming. Try folding napkins in different ways to give your table design a new dimension.

RIGHT: White table linens can withstand high wash temperatures and bleaching products, which means that, treated properly, they keep their pure, crisp finish.

Napkin Pockets

Tuck pastel napkins into organza sachets for pretty table settings. The sachets will keep newly laundered napkins clean when they are stored.

MATERIALS

58 x 15cm/23 x 6in   sewing kit

silk organza per sachet   tape measure

1 Turn in, press and stitch a double hem of 5mm/¼in on one short side of the organza.

2 Starting at the hem, measure 24cm/9in down the length of the fabric, fold at this point with wrong sides together and press. Stitch the sides in place, taking a 5mm/¼in seam. Trim the raw edges close to the stitching.

3 Turn the sachet inside out and stitch again over the side seams to encase the first seams.

4 To make the flap, turn under and stitch 5mm/¼in on the right side of the short raw edge. Fold the flap in half so that the hemmed edge meets the hem of the pocket. Stitch the side seams. Trim the stitching, turn right side out. Press and stitch the hemmed edge in place.

STAIN-FREE TABLE LINENS

Mop up spills immediately, then wash stained fabrics as soon as possible before the stains have chance to dry.

• Blot red wine before it dries with a cloth; then soak it up with a sprinkling of salt.

• Scrape off cold candle wax using a blunt knife, then place the cloth between layers of absorbent paper and iron with a hot iron. The wax will melt and disperse into the paper – replace with new paper as soon as it is saturated, or you may iron the stain back into the fabric.

• Briefly soak beer or lager stains in a mild white-wine vinegar solution, then wash.

• If after several washes white pure linen or cotton cloths are still stained, soak them in a bleach solution (1 tbsp to 1litre/1¾ pints/4 cups water) before washing with an all-white laundry load.

ABOVE: Soft modern fabrics give table settings a relaxed appearance. Less formal contemporary dining means we can take advantage of an enormous variety of easy-care woven fabrics. Inexpensive to buy and easy to launder, these table linens make a brilliant, time-saving choice for today's busy lifestyle.

China & Porcelain

Everyday china is robust and usually made to withstand the rigours of the dishwasher, but fine china items, especially older pieces, need to be handled with some care to preserve their good looks.

IT IS WORTH TAKING CARE of your fine china and porcelain pieces. They may be fragile, but if you treat them with respect they will give you years of service and enjoyment. Inherited bone china items are especially precious.

It is always safest to hand-wash good china. If you do want to use a dishwasher to save time, however, many models now include a 'china' or 'crystal' setting. Use a mild dishwasher detergent made for china. Never use abrasive pads on any type of china to remove dried or burnt-on food. Instead, soak the item in a mild detergent, overnight if necessary, then wipe it clean with a sponge.

When storing good china, insert a paper or cloth divider between plates to protect them, and never stack cups. Although it is safe to use china to warm food gently in the microwave, it is probably best to avoid using it for cooking dishes – instead use purpose-made containers.

RIGHT: For a cold first course, plates can be laid in advance, but for hot courses, warm plates in the oven and bring them to the table as they are needed.

RIGHT: Chunky earthenware is practical and robust for everyday use or outdoor entertaining. Set on a colourful tablecloth, it lends a relaxed Mediterranean feel to a simple country setting.

BELOW LEFT: Traditional tableware designs never date and are as popular today as ever – use hardwearing modern versions for every day, and keep your more precious pieces for special occasions.

BELOW RIGHT: You can mix and match, adapt and even adorn a dinner service to suit the mood and the occasion. A good way to mix pieces from different sets is to link them by colour. Or you can collect different pieces in white or cream, to create a great effect using pieces that were never designed to go together.

Sparkling Glasses

Glorious, reflective glass brings sparkle to every table. Polish glasses to a crystal-clear shine, then, if you like, dress them up for special occasions.

FORMAL GLASS SUITES include up to eight sizes, starting with the smallest for liqueurs and increasing in size for port, sherry, white wine, red wine, champagne, water and brandy. For less formal occasions there are likely to be a wine glass and a large water glass, often joined by a champagne flute. Liqueur, port or brandy glasses are usually brought to the table at the end of the meal. When buying glasses, choose generous sizes. Red wine and brandy glasses should be capacious, since their contents need to breathe.

Always hand-wash fine glass or crystal, as these can chip in a dishwasher and too hot a wash can leave them with a dulling bloom. Add 30ml/2 tbsp vinegar, or a spoonful of baking powder to the final rinsing water to make glass gleam. When washing everyday glass in a dishwasher add a water softener to keep it smear-free.

RIGHT: To remove stains from narrow-necked decanters, half-fill them with warm water and add washing-up liquid (dishwashing detergent) with a handful of rice. Swirl around and the rice will clean off the stains without leaving any abrasions or scratch marks.

Heart-frosted Glasses

Frosting glasses is quick and easy. The frosting stays in place surprisingly firmly, and can be washed off in hot soapy water at the end of the party.

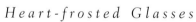

MATERIALS

1 beaten egg white
caster (superfine)
sugar
artist's paintbrush
off-white ribbon for
bows

1 Paint a motif on to each glass using a fine artist's brush dipped into plenty of beaten egg white.

2 Sprinkle the sugar on to the glass. It will stick to the egg white.

3 Dip the rim of the glass into the egg white, then into the sugar.

4 Add a ribbon bow to the stem, if you like.

ABOVE: Polish glass and lead crystal using a soft, lint-free cloth, just before you are going to use them. Hold the cloth in one hand and rotate the glass against it until it sparkles.

Store glasses in their original boxes, if you have them, to keep them from harm.

LEFT: When washing glasses, try adding baking powder to the rinsing water and leaving to drain. The glasses will dry to a smear-free shine.

Touching Wood

Furniture that gleams is a pleasure to look at. With regular care and polishing, the natural quality of the wood will be preserved and an attractive patina will develop.

MOST WOODEN FURNITURE is varnished, lacquered or waxed. Polishing wood will help to nourish it, but don't use sprays or liquid containing silicone or acrylic resin on antique wood. Beeswax is the best polish to use and will have been used on old furniture to build up an attractive patina. Apply the polish and buff in the direction of the grain using a clean soft cloth or duster. Oiled wood has a soft, low sheen and should not be polished. Instead, apply a wood oil sparingly with a soft cloth. Rub in the direction of the grain and gently buff using a clean soft cloth. With new furniture, apply two coats over a week, then oil twice a year. Danish and teak oil provide protection against water and food stains so are a good choice for kitchen surfaces.

Dust waxed and French-polished furniture daily and treat with a good wax polish from time to time. In between, buff with rolled chamois leather. Polished wood won't thrive in an atmosphere that is too warm or dry, or in direct sunlight, which bleaches it. Avoid placing it next to a window or radiator and introduce plants, vases of flowers or bowls of water into the room, but not directly on the piece itself. Remove water and heat marks by rubbing with the cut kernel of a Brazil nut or walnut. Stubborn stains can sometimes be removed using butter and cigarette ash; allow the mixture to soak in, then polish off.

RIGHT: Clean antiques with care, as damaging the patina can reduce the value – don't try to remove a stain if this will damage the patina. Remove grubby marks using a damp soft cloth and a little liquid soap. Wipe with a clean damp cloth. When dry, polish with natural beeswax, then buff gently to a shine. Deep scratch marks can be filled in using a coloured wax stick.

ABOVE: Painted
wooden furniture is
easy to keep clean. Dust
it with a damp cloth, or
use a solution of mild,
non-abrasive detergent
and water. Apply to one
section at a time, rinse
with clear water and dry
quickly with a cloth
before you continue.
Never use oil-based
products on painted
wooden furniture.

RIGHT: In the past,
butlers kept beeswax,
turpentine, essential oils
and dried lavender in
their store cupboards for
making furniture polish
and other cleaning
agents. Lavender was
valued for its disinfectant
qualities and its perfume,
so became a popular
ingredient for all kinds of
cleaning products.

Scented Beeswax &
Turpentine Furniture Polish

*Old-fashioned polish gives furniture a deep glowing shine that's hard to
achieve with modern sprays. It's well worth the effort to make your own.*

INGREDIENTS

75g/3oz block
natural beeswax
200ml/7fl oz/scant
1 cup pure turpentine
20 drops lavender oil
20 drops cedarwood oil
10 drops sandalwood oil

1 Grate the beeswax and place the shavings in a large
screw-top glass jar. Working in a well-ventilated room,
carefully pour the turpentine over the beeswax. Screw
on the lid and leave in a cool, dark place for a week,
stirring occasionally until the mixture becomes a
smooth cream.

2 Add the essential oils to the beeswax cream mixture
and mix in well. The polish is now ready for use.

Cutlery & Candelabra

Shiny silver and stainless steel cutlery brings an element of sculpture to the dining table. Sterling silver-plated cutlery does require more care than stainless steel, but grandma's time-honoured secrets will help keep it dazzling.

WASH SILVER CUTLERY as soon as possible after use in warm soapy water, as salt, vinegar, lemon juice and egg can damage the surface. Remove debris with a soft brush. Rinse and dry by hand, using a soft cloth to remove any watermarks. Store silver in a cutlery tray or baize-lined box, to prevent scratches.

Traditionally, if cutlery became tarnished, it was left to soak for a few hours in a bowl of water, with a handful of salt and some crumpled foil. Modern proprietary silver cleaners do the job more quickly; the best are rubbed on and either rinsed or polished off almost immediately. Silver cutlery and decorations that are left in 'dip' products soon lose their shine, but if you want to use a dip product, use it to dampen a cotton bud (swab), then gently wipe the silver to remove the tarnish. Rinse thoroughly, and buff to dry.

Kitchen knives require slightly different treatment. Whether they are stainless steel or carbon steel, wash and dry them as soon as possible after use, as food can discolour and pit the surface of the blade. It is best to hand-wash cook's cutlery: the blades can prove a hazard, and the handles can loosen in the dishwasher over time. It is particularly important to dry carbon blades immediately, since they soon become rusted. A little cooking oil wiped on to the clean dry blades will help to protect them. If a blade does become rusted, rub it as soon as possible with an abrasive cloth, then wash and dry.

RIGHT: A traditional technique for silver cutlery is to prepare a jar of soapy water and plunge the cutlery into it after each course, keeping bone or other fixed-on handles above the waterline, or they will loosen. After soaking, wash off any debris that remains.

RIGHT: Candelabra are an excellent way of creating a special atmosphere on more formal occasions, by allowing the diners to eat surrounded by soft candlelight instead of under harsh electric lights. Try to remove dripped candle wax from silver candelabra as soon as possible. If the wax has hardened, immerse the candlestick briefly in hot water to soften it again. Then pick off the wax and dry the silver quickly to prevent watermarks from spoiling its appearance.

RIGHT: Antique and modern styles can look striking when placed together on the table, and will reduce the amount of hand-washing required. Here, translucent acrylic-handled cutlery brings colour to the table, setting off the elegant antique silver.

ABOVE For a modern table setting, float tiny candles with flowers in a bowl of water.

BELOW: Available in a multitude of designs, candlesticks provide a dramatic way to display candles. If they become grubby, immerse in warm soapy water and work an old make-up, shaving or toothbrush into any awkward crevices.

The Linen Press

Time-honoured practices ensure your clothes

and linens always look good and smell fresh

and sweet. Beautiful old fabrics, handed

down through the family or

found in an antique shop, can also

continue to give good service.

A well-ordered wardrobe of cared-for clothes is a pleasure to behold. It's a principle that was well understood in the days when garments were expected to last considerably longer than the couple of seasons that's desired of them nowadays. But even if fashion seasons change rather more rapidly these days, classic pieces can become perennial favourites and serve you well for years, so it is as well to keep them looking fresh and new for as long as possible.

The key is to keep all garments laundered, and not to put them away soiled, as long-term stains can damage the fibres of the fabric. With the combination of a choice of wash programmes on modern machines, excellent stain removers (traditional and modern), and in-wash soakers and detergents, this has never been easier. The international laundry code makes laundry mistakes far less common. Some good-quality natural fibres can withstand, and often benefit from, very hot washes;

The simplest ideas are often the most effective. These lavender-filled sachets have been decorated with rows of buttons and toning velvet ribbon, to make elegant, decorative drawer scenters.

indeed, in days gone by, white cottons were boiled to ensure efficient stain removal.

Line drying, preferably outdoors, is the most natural and economic way of drying clothes – tumble dryers use a lot of energy and excessive heat can shrink, crease or melt fibres. You can stretch an indoor clothesline across the laundry room or across the bath. Synthetic and wool sweaters, which can become misshapen, need to be dried carefully. Indoors, lay them flat on a rack suspended over the bath. Outdoors, thread a pair of old tights (pantyhose) through the arms, pegging them at the wrist and neck holes. Hang shirts from two hangers, with the hooks facing so that they will not be blown off the washing line.

Drying laundry outside on the line helps to ease out large creases.

Keep a sewing kit to hand, so loose buttons can quickly be restored.

Freshly laundered bed linen is inviting and relaxing. Washing softens the fibres of old linen sheeting, making it more comfortable with age.

Fold newly laundered clothes carefully before storing them in drawers scented with easy-to-make herb sachets.

Freshly ironed shirts, blouses and bed linen look good and feel even better. Press delicate fabrics, wool and pleated materials by lowering the iron lightly on to the fabric. Iron cotton, bed linens, polyester and silk by gliding the iron smoothly up and down. Always check the care label for the recommended temperature. Avoid shine on bulky areas, such as a thick seam or zip (zipper), by pressing over a cloth, and iron bulky fabric, such as denim and canvas, inside-out, especially if it is dark. Iron silk damp and using a pressing cloth to prevent shiny patches. Place embroidered silk face down on to a white towel to make the embroidery stand out.

The way you store linen and garments can affect their useful life. Knitted fabrics are best folded and stored flat on a shelf. Jackets and dresses should be hung up, preferably on padded hangers; skirts and trousers should be placed on suitable expanding hangers. The wardrobe should not be over-crowded, as you need to allow air to circulate around the garments. Protection against moths always used to be a priority, and while synthetic fibres are less inviting to moths, natural fibres are still vulnerable. Lavender is a traditional natural defence against insects, and is blessed with a perfume that is desirable in any wardrobe.

Perfumed Closets

Sweetly scented drawers, wardrobes and shelves bring a delicate, natural perfume to freshly laundered clothes and household linens. Choose natural fragrances for best effect.

AROMATIC HERBS AND SPICES make exquisite ingredients for home-made drawer scenters. They are more pleasing than ready-made drawer liners, which are often impregnated with synthetic perfumes. Up to the 17th century, lavender was used in chests of drawers and linen presses to overcome the rancid smell of soap, which had yet to be perfumed. It has long been the most popular herb for scenting wardrobes and drawers, valued both for its exquisite perfume and its insect-deterrent properties. Nowadays, we still use it, as well as other herbs and spices, to add fresh, natural scent to newly laundered clothes. Spices, such as cardamom, cassia bark and cinnamon, make exotic alternatives. It doesn't take long to make up a few pretty sachets to place in drawers or hang in cupboards.

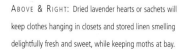

ABOVE & RIGHT: Dried lavender hearts or sachets will keep clothes hanging in closets and stored linen smelling delightfully fresh and sweet, while keeping moths at bay.

Aromatic Padded Hanger

Delicate non-stretch fabrics that should not be tumble-dried are best hung up to dry.
Using a padded hanger will avoid pushing shoulders out of shape. These have been filled with
cassia bark, to lend the clothes an exotic aroma.

MATERIALS

polyester wadding
(batting)
sewing kit
wooden coat hangers
75mm/3in-wide satin
ribbon
dressmaker's pins
cassia bark
selection of organza,
petersham or grosgrain
and embroidered
ribbons

Lavender Bottles

These delightful, traditional drawer scenters are a
little fiddly to make but well worth the effort.
The best effect is obtained by using lavender with
long stems and large blooms.

MATERIALS

For each bottle:	*fine string*
9 *(or any odd number)*	*approximately 1m/1yd*
stalks of fresh lavender	*ribbon*

1 Tightly tie an odd number of lavender stalks together, at the base of the blooms, using fine string.

2 Tie a ribbon to the top of one stalk just below the flowers. Hold the lavender flowers, then bend the stalks down, one by one, over the flowers. Be careful not to snap the stalks.

3 Weave the ribbon in and out of the lavender stalks, keeping the ribbon flat and forming a gently rounded shape over the flowerheads. When you have covered the flowers, knot the ribbon ends.

1 Cut a strip of wadding for each hanger. Wind it around the hanger and secure with stitches. Cut a rectangle of wadding to cover both sides of the hanger. Stitch in place, adding the cassia bark, then tuck in the ends.

2 Cut two lengths of 75mm/3in-wide satin ribbon to make the cover for the hanger. With right sides together, stitch the ends together, shaping the stitching into a gentle curve to fit the hanger ends. Stitch along one long edge and turn right side out. Fit the cover over the hanger and slip stitch in place.

3 To make a rose, fold a tiny piece of wadding into the end of a length of organza ribbon and secure with a stitch. Fold and wind the rest of the ribbon around this central bud, stitching through the layers to secure. Tuck in the raw edge. Make two roses for each hanger.

4 To make a rosette, cut a length of ribbon 12.5cm/5in long and stitch the raw edges together. Work running stitch around the ribbon to one side of the centre. Pull up and secure. Make two rosettes for each hanger.

5 Make a leaf from a short length of green ribbon. Fold in the short ends to make a V shape. Work running stitch along this raw edge and pull up the gathers. Make four leaves. Tie a ribbon bow around the centre of each hanger. Add the leaves and flowers to it.

Laundering Lore

There's something immensely satisfying about transforming an unruly jumble of dirty laundry into a fresh,
sweet-smelling pile, ready to be tucked into drawers, stacked on shelves and hung in wardrobes.

M ODERN TECHNOLOGY, efficient washing products and
steam-assisted irons have turned the traditional washday
into a relative breeze. Follow the care system printed on garment
labels and take heed of a few of grandma's tips.

Sort laundry into separate piles of similar colours and whites,
and similar fabric types that use the same wash cycle. Turn
clothes inside out as this reduces wear on the outer finish, and
is important with clothes such as knitted garments, which
might pill. Treat stains as soon as possible and keep a stain-
removal kit handy: clean white cloths to soak up spills and apply
cleaner; spray pre-wash liquid, a detergent soap bar and liquid
biological detergent; methylated spirits (denatured alcohol) for
grass stains on colourfast fabric; glycerine
(diluted with water for soaking up to one
hour) to soften dried-in stains; nail-polish
remover (not for acetates); hydrogen
peroxide (20-volume strength mixed 1:9
with water) for soaking; white spirit (paint
thinner) for grease or fresh paint; white-
wine vinegar to neutralize odours, pet
stains and perspiration marks; borax to
neutralize acid stains such as wine, juice
and coffee.

RIGHT: Historically, artisans and those who worked
on the land wore smocks, to keep their clothing clean
while they worked.

RIGHT: In 19th-century
America, in the summer
months, the Shaker
people used to dry their
clothes and household
linen on lavender bushes
to impregnate the fabric
with the delicious scent of
the flowers. The most
fragrant time is just after
the dew has dried and
before the sun is too hot.

STAIN-FREE LAUNDRY

Treat a stain as soon as possible to prevent it becoming permanent, blotting excess with a clean cloth or salt to stop it spreading.

- For adhesives: Dab superglues immediately with a little lighter fuel. Remove other glues with amyl acetate, which is available from chemists (drugstores).
- For blood: Rinse under cold water and soak in a solution of biological washing liquid and tepid water. Soak white garments in a mild ammonia and water solution, then wash.
- For chewing gum: Chill the garment in the refrigerator, then pick off the hardened gum. Dab with methylated spirits or dry-cleaning fluid.
- For crayon: Dab the affected area with white spirit, and use a heavy-duty detergent containing oxygen bleach for the remainder of the fabric.
- For fats, grease and cooking oil: Dampen with water and apply a heavy-duty liquid detergent. Wash immediately in the hottest water the fabric will stand.
- For ink: Dab ballpoint pen with nail-polish remover. Cover blue and black fountain pen with salt and lemon juice. Rinse and wash with biological liquid detergent.

- For lipstick: Dab with white spirit, work a liquid detergent into the fibres, then hot-wash.
- For perspiration: Dab with a solution of 1 part white-wine vinegar to 10 parts water.
- For shoe polish: Dab with a grease solvent or methylated spirit. Soak in a strong detergent solution, then wash.

UNDERSTANDING THE WASHCARE SYMBOLS

 This number indicates the recommended centigrade temperature. A higher temperature could shrink or discolour the garment.

 A line under the tub indicates a gentler action, usually used for synthetics; two lines indicates a wool wash or delicate cycle.

 A hand symbol is for hand-wash garments.

 A crossed-out wash tub means that the garment is not suitable for washing. It is usually positioned next to a dry cleaning symbol.

 If a circle is crossed out, this means do not dry clean the garment – the process may destroy the fibres and damage the garment's shape . Other circles show letters A or P and some show a bar underneath. These advise the cleaner which solvents to use.

 A circle in a square indicates that an item can be tumble dried. If it is crossed out this means that tumble drying may cause damage to the garment. A single dot inside the circle indicates that you should dry on a low heat setting; two dots means that a high setting can be used.

 A T-shirt in a square means dry the garment flat, away from direct heat. It is used for garments which can easily be pulled out of shape.

 The iron symbol will show one, two or three dots, which indicates the appropriate iron temperature. The more dots it shows, the higher the setting. A crossed-out iron means that the item should not be ironed.

 A triangle (sometimes with the letters CI inside) indicates that chlorine bleach can be used; a crossed-out triangle means you should not use bleach.

New Life for Linen & Lace

Beautiful old linens and lace, often exquisitely detailed with hand embroidery or drawn-thread work, are a wonderful alternative to modern fabrics. With the right attention, these durable materials offer many years of service.

ANTIQUE FABRICS were manufactured from best-quality fibres and made to last, and over the years they have softened with use – a quality that only seems to add to their appeal. They take more time and attention to care for when laundered, but the effort is worthwhile.

Their timeless charm can be combined with modern fabrics to create an overall effect of luxury and old-fashioned good taste. They make extremely comfortable bed linen and beautiful table linen. Small pieces, cut from the edges of worn sheets, can be recycled as pretty handkerchiefs edged with lace, charming nightdress cases or laundry bags for use when travelling. Secondhand finds with lots of decorative details, such as whitework embroidery, lace and drawn-thread work are well worth buying, and if treated with the necessary care they should last for many more years.

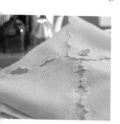

ABOVE & RIGHT: Antique natural fabrics are strong and long-lasting. Decorative versions are much sought after.

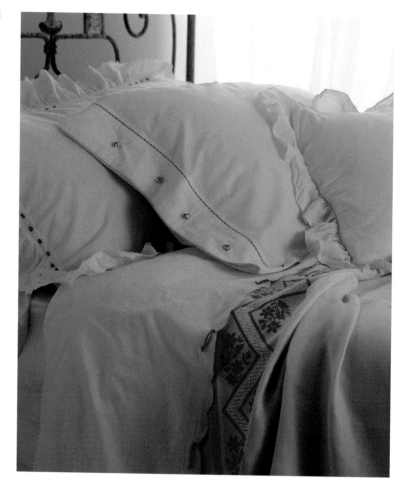

RIGHT: Soak linens in a solution of gentle detergent or proprietary soaking agent, overnight or longer. Machine wash on a gentle cycle with a mild detergent, then rinse thoroughly by hand, adding half a cup of white vinegar to the rinsing water. Any remaining stains on white linens should be treated either with pure lemon juice or a paste of lemon juice and salt, applied to damp fabric. Then, if possible, leave to dry on the lawn for a day (or even two), dampening the fabric if necessary. However improbable this sounds, experts swear that the sunlight, interacting with water and chlorophyll in the grass, works wonders for white linens.

Pure linen is known for stubborn creasing, and should be ironed using a steam iron at the hottest setting. Loosely fold or roll before storing.

BELOW: Clean lace by sprinkling with powdered magnesia, talcum powder or fine white kaolin. After a few days, rinse, soak overnight in soaking agent, then hand-wash, adding a little vinegar to the final rinse. For stains, dampen, then apply lemon juice before washing. Iron lace on a fluffy towel, and store in a pillowcase.

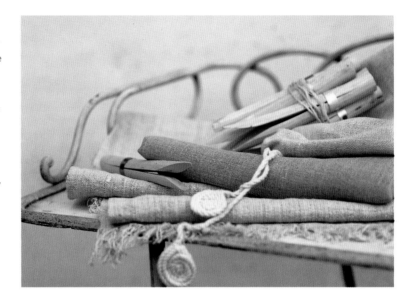

Drawstring Bags

These simple drawstring bags, made from scraps of decorative fabric, are useful for holding shoes, small laundry items, underwear or small accessories.

MATERIALS

2 rectangles of fabric,	length of lace trim
decorated with beads	ribbon or cord
or embroidery	sewing kit

1 Place the rectangles right sides together. Using 1cm/½in seams, stitch down one long edge, across one short edge and up the other long edge. Leave a 2.5cm/1in gap in the stitching 2.5cm/1in from the short raw edges to form the channel to thread the cord through.

2 Turn in, press and stitch the raw edges of the bag opening. Trim all the seams and seal the raw edges with zigzag stitch.

3 Turn right side out. Turn in 7.5cm/3in at the open edge and press. Stitch the lace trim to the folded edge. Stitch around each side of the 2.5cm/1in opening to form a channel. Thread the cord through the channel.

A Stitch in Time

Even if sewing is not your strong point, there are times when a little attention can prolong the life of a favourite garment or piece of furnishing. And there is a certain satisfaction to be gained in doing the job successfully.

notice a stray thread poking out from a needle-hole in a button, it's a sure sign the whole lot will soon unravel. Check all the other buttons, because more often than not they will all soon follow their leader. Keep a small sewing kit near your wardrobe so that you can restore a loose button when you're getting dressed in the morning. Hems can take longer to mend, so these need to be put aside for stitching later when you have more time.

Torn fabric represents more of a problem as cut edges fray so easily. Thankfully, nowadays we have the advantage of iron-on patches. Iron them on to the inside of the garment.

WHILE THERE AREN'T MANY of us who would want to return to the days of turning frayed collars and cuffs or cutting worn sheets in half to stitch sides-to-middle, there are some repairs we do have to undertake from time to time.

The old adage 'a stitch in time saves nine' is undeniably true, so it is wise to keep up with repairs on clothing as soon as you notice the need for them. If you sew on a button while it's still hanging loose, for example, you won't find yourself several months later having to replace the lot because you can't find a match for the one that has gone missing. The next time you

ABOVE & RIGHT: The most basic sewing kit – scissors, needles, pins, thread, spare buttons and fabric scraps for patches – is all you need. The trick is to have it near at hand so you can make repairs immediately. Carry a mini version in your handbag.

ABOVE: Old clothes were once recycled into patchwork quilts to prolong the useful life of the fabric.

ABOVE: Use colourful machine-embroidery threads to add embellishments to fabrics.

Depending on the position of the tear and the type of fabric, can make a secure, invisible mend. Holes in the knees of children's trousers need a robust mend. While children are young, this is easy to do using patches or appliqué. You could fix an iron-on patch on the inside, then add an appealing motif to the outside.

Growing children are more likely to tear their clothes. They also go through alarming growth spurts. If fringes, frays and trimmings are in fashion, let them help choose some they like and sew them to hems to prolong the life of a garment for a few more months. If children refuse to contemplate such strategies, you may be able to lengthen the garment's life by letting the hem down. If you think you might need to do this, hang dresses and skirts inside out so the sun has a chance to fade the inside of the hem to match the rest of the garment when it's time to lengthen.

Worn edges of any fabric item, whether on garments, linens, curtains, or even quilts, are easy to deal with by cutting away the worn edge and applying a new binding or contrasting fabric edging. Depending on the binding you choose you can give an old favourite a new fashion life at the sime time as prolonging its use: a favourite fine knitted jumper, for example, could be glamorously updated using a broad velvet ribbon; curtains could be renewed with a band of contrasting colour at the bottom and sides and a blouse could be fitted with picot-edged braid down a worn button band.

Motif Patches

Why not appliqué a charming motif to a patch to cover a tear? Add machine or hand embroidery to the motif, if you like. The child will be delighted and the garment will give several months' extra wear. Here, a bird has been used, but you can use any motif.

MATERIALS
fabric scraps for the appliqué motif and patch
fusible webbing
stranded embroidery thread (floss)
sewing kit

1 Cut one patch large enough to cover the tear.
2 Make a template for each part of the motif: a body, a wing, two legs and a heart. Cut one of each from fusible webbing.
3 Fuse each shape to the wrong side of contrasting fabrics, then cut out each shape. Fuse the heart to the wing, the wing to the bird, and the bird and legs to the patch.
4 Using embroidery thread (floss), stab stitch around the bird and legs. Stitch around the heart, sew on an eye.

Scenting the Room

Nature's own perfumes lend a fresh, seasonal aroma to each room, while bestowing a general sense of wellbeing.
So make your own pot-pourri and bring flowers and foliage in from outside.

A SWEETLY SCENTED HOME is an immediately welcoming one. The power of perfumes has been appreciated since ancient times, but often for different reasons than today. In the Middle Ages it was thought that 'bad odours' were the cause of diseases such as the plague, and doctors carried posies of lavender and other sweet-smelling flowers to ward off infection. Lavender was also used to fumigate sick areas. Although few people would now suggest using sweet-smelling flowers to guard against seriously infectious diseases, contemporary aromatherapists do believe that odours can affect chemical balances in the brain. This could account for the mood-changing properties of many herbs, and some scented herbs, flowers and spices can actually promote a feeling of wellbeing. Natural perfumes are infinitely more satisfying than synthetic ones, so bring scents in from the outside. There are many ways to do this, using seasonal flowers and foliage, as well as natural home-made pot-pourris.

LEFT: The fragrance of freshly cut flowers can fill an entire room.

LEFT: Fresh or dried, in simple or elaborate arrangements, lavender brings a wonderful scent to the home. Floors were once sprinkled with lavender flowers to scent the room and mask odours.

Summer Pot-pourri

Make the summer's scent last all year long by harvesting garden blooms and turning them into pot-pourri. Garden lavender can be dried by hanging bunches upside down in an airy room. Roses, with their dense petal arrangement, need to be desiccated. Place them in a box of silica gel (from a good pharmacy) or fine sand and cover with more desiccant, then seal the box for up to 10 days. You'll also need essential oils to strengthen the perfumes to make the aromas longer-lasting and fixatives.

INGREDIENTS

6ml/120 drops
lavender essential oil
5ml/100 drops
geranium essential oil
25g/1oz ground
orris root
15g/½oz whole cloves

15g/½oz dried mace
115g/4oz dried
lavender
225g/8oz dried rose
petals
225g/8oz dried
rosebuds

ABOVE: Pomanders and scented sachets have always been used to keep clothing and linen insect-free and smelling fresh, but if you make them with beautiful fabrics in pretty designs, you can hang them on the outside of wardrobe door handles or over the corner of a small picture to scent the room.

1 Measure out the essential oils into a small bottle and shake well. Add a few drops to the ground orris root and stir to create a crumbly mixture.

2 Add the remainder of the blended oils to the cloves and mace and mix well. Cover and leave in a dark place for 24 hours to allow the fragrances to mingle.

3 Mix the dried flowers and petals in a large bowl using a wooden spoon. Add the dried spice mixture and mix. Add the orris root mixture and stir well again. Cover and leave in a dark place for up to six weeks to allow the scents to mingle.

4 To display, arrange in a non-porous container.

LEFT: Use a vaporizer to disperse your favourite essential oils around a room. Vaporizers have a bowl or saucer to hold water and oil and usually have space below to hold a tealight. The heat from the candle warms the oil and water and as they evaporate they scent the air.

BAGNO SCHIUMA

ALLA CALENDULA

indicato per pelli sensibili

Body & Soul

Discover the secrets of the stillrooms of old

and benefit from pure hand-made soaps,

luxurious bath additives and healing

treatments made from

traditional, natural and

scented ingredients.

Pampering Treats

Treat yourself, friends and family to exquisite hand-made soaps, scrubs and lotions that are free from synthetic perfumes and drying additives. Scented with the purest essential oils, they also offer healing benefits.

A LONG SOAK IN A warm bath, lathering with fine soap, is an everyday indulgence we can all enjoy. The purest hand-made soaps, which are gentle on the skin, are now increasingly available. However, it's not difficult to make your own, using traditional methods that country people relied on right into the 20th century. Body scrubs are simple to make, too, and provide an invigorating method of deeper cleansing. You can also make a refreshing body lotion. If your limbs and muscles ache after a hard day, relax with a chamomile massage oil.

RIGHT: A collection of essential oils will prove invaluable for making up your favourite home preparations.

RIGHT: Hand-milled lemongrass soap makes a wonderful present, especially if packaged in papyrus paper and raffia. Finely grate a 150g/5oz bar of unscented soap into a heatproof bowl. Add water in the proportion of one part water to two parts soap. Put the bowl over a pan of simmering water, stir the mixture continuously until it coalesces, and remove from the heat. Tip the soap into a mortar, add 12 drops of lemongrass oil, and mix well with a pestle. Wet your hands, and work the mixture into two bars. Leave on a wooden board to dry out and set hard, which may take a couple of days. Use within a month.

Geranium Body Lotion

Geranium oil has an exquisite, slightly spicy yet floral fragrance that makes it a
wonderful addition to any home-made lotion. You can use this versatile lotion to
rehydrate dry skin in cold winter months and to cool the effects of
sunburn in summer.

INGREDIENTS

1.5ml/¼ tsp borax
5ml/1 tsp white beeswax
5ml/1 tsp lanolin
30ml/2 tbsp petroleum jelly
25ml/1½ tbsp apricot kernel
oil
20ml/4 tsp almond oil
20 drops geranium oil

1 In a bowl, dissolve the borax in 30ml/2 tbsp boiled water. Set aside.

2 Put the beeswax, lanolin and petroleum jelly with the apricot kernel and almond oils in a bowl. Set this over a pan of gently simmering water until the wax melts. Stir well to blend. Remove the bowl from the heat.

3 Add the borax solution, whisking as the lanolin thickens and turns white. Continue whisking until the mixture is cool.

4 Stir the geranium oil into the cooled mixture, then pour the lotion into a glass bottle. Seal when cold and store in a dark place. The mixture will keep for a few weeks, so make it in small batches.

RIGHT: With its soothing and relaxing properties, chamomile is a wonderful ingredient for a massage oil that can be used to ease the strains of a long, hard day. Pour 45ml/ 3 tbsp almond oil and 5ml/1 tsp wheatgerm oil into a glass bottle, add 10 drops chamomile oil and shake well to mix thoroughly. Store the oil in a cool place away from the light. Massage tired limbs and aching muscles with the scented oil before bed.

ABOVE: Body scrubs stimulate the circulation and are perfect for reviving winter-weary skin. The rough texture of the dry ingredients helps to exfoliate the skin and draw out any impurities. Massage into the skin in small circular movements, adding a little water if necessary. Rinse off with warm water. Pat the skin dry with a warm towel.

Bathtime Fragrances

Indulge in bathtime pleasure by using gloriously perfumed and therapeutic bath oils, bubble bath, bath salts and scented flower petals to help soak away the day's stresses.

SINKING INTO A WARM BATH scented with fragrant oils or full of soft foam bubbles is one of the simplest yet most seductive of luxuries. The steamy warmth of the bath alone is associated with all the sensuality and symbolism of the sybaritic pleasures. By adding aromatic bath oils, which hydrate the skin as they envelop you in their heady perfume, you are creating an environment for relaxation and privacy, and a quiet time to contemplate.

Many essential oils affect the mind and emotions and can be used in a positive way to enhance your well-being. An early morning bath should contain scents that invigorate and energize, putting you in a frame of mind to greet the day. A bath in the evening should contain gentle relaxing scents that promote sleep, such as lavender.

RIGHT: Add bath foam while the water is running, but add oils once the bath is full and the water is still, just before you step in, or the essential oils will evaporate into the surrounding air instead of adhering to your skin with the carrier oil.

Sandalwood & Rose Bath Oil

Rose and sandalwood essential oils have an undeniably sensuous fragrance. Rose oil is very powerful and a little will go a long way. When combined with sandalwood oil, it creates a warm, spicy fragrance that will remain on the skin long after your bath. This is an effective treatment for dry skin.

INGREDIENTS

100ml/3½ fl oz almond oil

20ml/4 tsp wheatgerm oil

15 drops rose oil

10 drops sandalwood oil

1 Measure out the almond and wheatgerm oils and pour into a dark glass bottle.

2 Add the rose and sandalwood oils and shake to mix.

ABOVE: For delicately scented bath water, put a handful of herbs in a linen bag. Tie it around the tap so that the water flows through the contents when filling the bath.

Reviving Rose Bath Salts

A bath containing a combination of salt, aromatic dried rose petals and essential oils is wonderfully invigorating, lifts the spirits and scents the skin.

INGREDIENTS

10g/¼oz dried rose petals

450g/1lb coarse sea salt

10 drops rose geranium oil

5 drops lavender oil

5 drops bergamot oil

1 Using a mortar and pestle, grind all but a handful of the dried rose petals to a fine powder. Mix into the salt. Add the remaining ingredients, stirring with each addition.

2 Spoon the bath salts into a decorative jar with a close-fitting lid.

Skin Care

Treat yourself to home-made skin preparations made from pure natural ingredients, and enjoy their beneficial effects and exquisite perfumes.

MAKING YOUR OWN COSMETICS is a real pleasure and there are plenty of rewards. Once you've mastered the basic techniques, you'll be able to create alternative consistencies and perfumes to suit your own skin. Additionally, you'll know your cosmetics include only pure ingredients. And when you use fresh herbs and essential oils, there will be many therapeutic benefits.

Although herbs and essential oils are natural ingredients, they can produce strong results. Lavender and tea-tree oil are the only essential oils that are safe to use on the skin undiluted – others need to be treated with respect. Always test a small amount of a home-made cosmetic on the inside of your arm and check for any reactions in the first 24 hours before using it on your face. The treatments shown here are made with mild ingredients and should suit most skins.

ABOVE RIGHT: Since home-made cosmetics are free from preservatives, they don't have the same shelf life as commercial ones, so make them up in small batches. Keep them in the refrigerator and use within one month.

Chamomile Steam Facial

The heat in steam treatments opens the pores, releasing any impurities and boosting the blood circulation. Chamomile adds a gentle cleansing action that is suitable for most skins.

INGREDIENTS

*40g/1½oz fresh or
15g/½oz dried
chamomile flowers
600ml/1 pint/2½cups
boiling water*

1 In a pan, make an infusion of the chamomile and boiling water. Leave to stand for 30 minutes, then strain.
2 Re-heat the infusion and pour it into a large, heatproof bowl. Keeping your face about 30cm/12in above the steam, drape a towel over your head and the bowl and keep covered for about 30 seconds.

Comfrey & Rosewater Mask

This nourishing face mask will tighten the skin, help to heal blemishes and refine open pores. It is ideal for dry skin.

INGREDIENTS

6 comfrey leaves	*1 egg yolk*
150ml/¼ pint/⅔ cup	*5ml/1 tsp honey*
boiling water	*5ml/1 tsp rosewater*
30ml/2 tbsp fine	*5 drops wheatgerm oil*
oatmeal	*natural (plain) yogurt*

1 Add the comfrey to the boiling water and leave to cool before straining. Mix 15ml/1 tbsp of this infusion with the other ingredients to make a smooth paste.

2 Apply evenly to the face, avoiding the eye area. Leave for 10–15 minutes, then rinse off.

BELOW: Dusting powders can be tailor-made. To a base of 30ml/5 tbsp unscented talc, add 15ml/1 tbsp of cornflour (cornstarch) and 5 drops of your favourite essential oil.

RIGHT: To make lavender moisturizer, put 20ml/4 tsp beeswax granules, 20g/¾ oz cocoa butter and 75ml/5 tbsp almond oil in a bowl set over a pan of simmering water and melt, stirring constantly. In a separate pan, dissolve 10ml/2 tsp borax in 175ml/6fl oz/¾ cup lavender water by gently warming it. Combine with the mixture in the bowl. Remove from the heat. While tepid, add 8 drops lavender oil and stir well. Allow to cool.

Healing Treatments

Take a tip from the medicine cabinets of yesteryear, and make up soothing balms, salves and ointments for bruised and chapped skin, or an old-fashioned vapour rub for clearing a blocked nose.

I N THE PAST, country dwellers knew how to make up salves and balms for chapped skin and lips, and liniments and embrocations for massaging into sprains and strains. A lip balm made with lavender, for example, can soothe lips chapped by sun, wind, weather or even illness. It is made by melting 5ml/1 tsp each of beeswax, cocoa butter and wheatgerm oil together, allowing them to cool for a few minutes then mixing in three drops of lavender essential oil. Pour the balm into a small jar and leave to set. Rosewater mixed into honey is also good for sore or chapped lips.

RIGHT: Calendula cream soothes skin irritations, from insect bites and sunburn to eczema and itchy allergic rashes. Pour 300ml/½ pint/1¼ cups boiling water over 15g/½ oz dried pot marigold petals (or 30g/1oz fresh), cover and leave to cool. Melt 60ml/4 tbsp emulsifying ointment with 15ml/1 tbsp glycerine, in a bowl set over simmering water. Remove from the heat and stir 4 drops of tincture of benzoin and 4–5 drops of calendula oil (optional) into 150ml/¼ pint/⅔ cup of the infusion. Stir until cooled and the consistency of thick cream. Transfer to a small jar before it sets.

Winter Hand Cream

This nourishing cream incorporates patchouli oil, which is a particularly good healer of cracked, chapped skin. Treat your hands to a generous application of cream at night, pull on some cotton gloves and, having absorbed all the cream overnight, your hands will feel softened and rejuvenated.

INGREDIENTS

75g/3oz unscented hard white soap	150ml/¼ pint/⅔ cup almond oil
115g/4oz beeswax	45ml/3 tbsp rosewater
45ml/3 tbsp glycerine	25 drops patchouli oil

1 Finely grate the soap into a heatproof bowl, pour over 90ml/6 tbsp boiling water and stir until smooth. In another heatproof bowl, combine the beeswax, glycerine, almond oil and rosewater, set over a pan of boiling water and melt over a gentle heat.

2 Remove from the heat and gradually whisk into the soap mixture. Keep whisking as the mixture cools and thickens. Stir in the patchouli oil and pour into jars.

Comfrey Bruise Ointment

The active ingredient in this ointment, comfrey helps to reduce bruising and ease sprains. It contains allantoin, which stimulates the growth of bone and soft tissue cells. Arnica, another excellent treatment for bruises and sprains, makes a good substitute for the comfrey, if necessary.

INGREDIENTS

200g/7oz petroleum jelly

30g/1oz fresh comfrey leaves, chopped

1 Put the petroleum jelly in a heatproof bowl set over a pan of boiling water, allow it to melt and add the chopped comfrey leaves. Stir well. Reduce the heat and leave the mixture over gently simmering water for about one hour.

2 Strain the mixture through muslin (cheesecloth) and pour immediately into a clean glass jar while still liquid. Leave to set, add a tight-fitting lid and keep in a cool, dark place.

LEFT: Lavender and eucalyptus make an aromatic vapour rub to keep the nose clear. Melt 50g/2oz petroleum jelly in a heatproof bowl over simmering water. Stir in 15ml/1 tbsp dried lavender and heat for 30 minutes. Strain through muslin (cheesecloth) and leave to cool slightly. Add 6 drops eucalyptus oil and 4 drops camphor oil. Pour into a clean jar and leave to set. Rub gently on to the throat, chest and back at bedtime.

Medicinal Remedies

The natural ingredients used in home remedies can provide welcome relief for common ailments. A surprising number of these remedies can be made from store-cupboard and garden ingredients.

IT WASN'T MUCH MORE than a couple of generations ago that country housewives depended entirely on their knowledge of herbal treatments for family coughs, colds and other common ailments. Women would collect and store ingredients for infusions and decoctions in their stillroom cupboards, ready for use. Some of the more simple remedies are very effective.

Gargling with an infusion of herbs, for instance, can ease a prickly throat. All you do is pour 600ml/1 pint/2½ cups of boiling water over a small handful each of fresh sage and thyme leaves, cover and leave for 30 mintues. Then strain and discard the leaves and stir into the liquid 30ml/2 tbsp cider vinegar, 10ml/2 tsp honey and 5ml/1 tsp cayenne. Substitute 30ml/2 tbsp dried herbs if fresh ones are unavailable. The gargle will keep for up to one week.

RIGHT: Many cold treatments can be made from store-cupboard ingredients; they can provide the perfect solution for fevers, which inevitably brew in the evening when all the pharmacies are closed.

Thyme & Borage Cough Linctus

Borage was traditionally used in cough syrup recipes, and thyme has antiseptic properties. Once bottled, this linctus will keep for at least two months. Take 5ml/1 tsp as required.

INGREDIENTS

25g/1oz fresh or 15g/½oz dried thyme
25g/1oz fresh or 15g/½oz dried borage
flowers and leaves
2 x 5cm/2in cinnamon sticks
600ml/1 pint/2½ cups water
juice of 1 small lemon
100g/4oz/½ cup honey

1 Put the herbs, cinnamon and water into a pan. Bring to the boil, cover and simmer for 20 minutes. Strain off the herbs and return the liquid to the pan. Simmer, uncovered, until reduced by half.
2 Add the lemon juice and honey and simmer gently for 5 minutes. Bottle and store in a cool place.

Ginger & Lemon Decoction

Soothe sore throats and ease the misery of winter colds with this warming decoction. The ginger encourages sweating to eliminate toxins and dispel mucus and catarrh. It will keep for two to three days. Drink a small cupful at a time, as needed.

INGREDIENTS

115g/4oz fresh root ginger, peeled and sliced
rind and juice of 1 lemon
pinch of cayenne pepper
600ml/1 pint/2½ cups water
honey, to taste

1 Put all the ingredients except the honey and lemon juice into a pan and bring to the boil. Cover and simmer for 20 minutes.
2 Remove from the heat, strain the liquid and add the lemon juice and honey.

ABOVE: Greek and Roman doctors prescribed garlic for respiratory infections, and modern research has confirmed its antibacterial, antiviral and decongestant properties. Combine a crushed head of garlic in a pan with 300ml/½ pint/1¼ cups of water. Bring to the boil and simmer for 20 minutes. Add the juice of half a lemon and 30ml/2 tbsp honey and simmer for 2–3 minutes. Allow the mixture to cool slightly, then strain it into a sterilized dark glass jar or bottle with an airtight lid. Store for up to 3 weeks in the refrigerator and take 10–15ml/ 2–3 tsp three times a day.

Flavoured Oils & Vinegars

*Oils and vinegars flavoured with delicious herbs or aromatic spices make tasty salad dressing
ingredients and lend extra piquancy to grilled and pan-fried food.*

CAPTURE THE ESSENCE of fresh herbs when they are at their peak in oils and vinegars to use as flavouring ingredients in your cooking. They are a real treat, so avoid cheap blended oils, and instead use good quality pure oils, such as sunflower, safflower, hazelnut or extra virgin olive oils, always buying the best that you can afford.

Most culinary herbs can be used to flavour oils, especially basil, fennel, marjoram, rosemary, sage, savory, tarragon and thyme. All these are good with vinegar, as also are chervil, dill, garlic, mint and rosemary.

Collect fresh herbs before they flower, in the morning, after the dew has dried but before the hot sun releases their flavours. Allow any moisture on the herbs to dry completely before use, otherwise they may become mouldy. Blot them between layers of kitchen paper if necessary.

RIGHT: You can add a token herb to flavoured oil or vinegar as identification, but remove it as soon as a bottle of oil is opened, or the oil may go rancid.

Adding Flavour

Pour the oil or vinegar into a wide-topped jar and add a large handful of herbs (making sure they are free from moisture). Allow to steep for 2 weeks, then strain and decant into a sterilized decorative bottle. If you like, add a sprig of the herbs to indicate the flavour, or write a label.

MIXED HERB VINEGAR

Steep sage, thyme, bay and marjoram in white wine vinegar, as above, then strain and decant. Tie a selection of herbs into a bunch and wind around with string before putting into the bottle.

TARRAGON VINEGAR

Steep tarragon in cider vinegar, as above, then strain and decant. Put two or three long sprigs of tarragon into the bottle.

MEDITERRANEAN HERB OIL

Steep rosemary, thyme and marjoram in extra virgin olive oil as above, strain and decant. Decorate with herbs tied around a cinnamon stick.

BASIL & CHILLI OIL

Steep basil and three chillies in extra virgin olive oil as above, then strain and decant. Put new basil sprigs and three chillies in the bottle to decorate.

FRUIT & FLOWER VINEGARS

These delicious vinegars make fragrant salad dressings and fruit salad ingredients. Make them by steeping and straining as above. To make raspberry vinegar, blackberry vinegar and rose petal vinegar, steep 115g/4oz raspberries, blackberries or rose petals in 600ml/1 pint/ 2½ cups cider vinegar, as above.

Spicy Olive Oil

Oil flavoured with freshly ground spices brings piquancy to any recipe. Make it in a similar way to herb oils, but fry the spices to release their flavours. Use the oil to pep up plain salad dressings, drizzle over bruschetta-style salads, fry steaks or chicken, or even as an instant marinade.

INGREDIENTS

30ml/2 tbsp coriander seeds

15ml/1 tbsp cumin seeds

15ml/1 tbsp cardamom pods

1 litre/1¾ pints/4 cups extra virgin olive oil

4 bay leaves, plus extra to decorate

1 Place the coriander and cumin seeds in a mortar and grind roughly with a pestle. Add the cardamom pods to the mortar and split them with the pestle.

2 Put all the spices in a pan. Dry-fry the spices over a high heat, but ensure that they do not burn.

3 Take the pan off the heat and add the oil. Pour into a large, sterilized screw-top jar or bottle. Add the bay leaves and allow to go completely cold before sealing the bottle tightly. Leave for 2 weeks in a cool, dark place, turning each day, to allow the flavours to develop.

4 Strain and decant into sterilized bottles. Add bay leaves to the bottle if you like, but as soon as the oil is used, the herbs must be removed immediately.

Preserved Fruits

Gather the best of the fruit that autumn has to offer, and transform it into delicious preserves to enjoy all through the winter. They can be eaten on their own or used as dessert ingredients.

WITH MODERN AIR-FREIGHTING we no longer have to rely on old-fashioned preserves for fruit in winter, but many traditional recipes are so wonderfully delicious they deserve to be made again and again.

Apples are excellent candidates for drying, and are simply rehydrated by soaking when required. In crystallized fruit, the natural water content is gradually replaced with sugar – cherries, plum, peaches, apricots, pineapples and pears are all good subjects. Gently poached fruit are bottled in their cooking syrup; the addition of brandy elevates them into something quite special. Fruit can be preserved in any distilled spirit – brandy, rum, whisky, gin or even vodka – and eaten as a dessert, or the liquid can be drunk as an after-dinner cordial. Even cheap spirit can produce good results.

RIGHT: Dried apples can be stored for several months. Slice them thinly and thread on to a wooden skewer. Place in a preheated oven set at a very low heat until dried out.

ABOVE: Slices of fruit, nuts and even small flowers can be preserved by being crystallized or coated in a boiled syrup made with sugar, water and vinegar. The process is time-consuming but well worth the effort for special occasions.

Cinnamon-spiced Cherries

These sumptuous fruits are delicious served with scoops of vanilla ice cream.

INGREDIENTS

500g/1lb 2oz/2½ cups granulated sugar	1kg/2¼lb cherries
3 cinnamon sticks	300ml/½ pint/ 1¼ cups brandy
4 star anise	

1 Put 300ml/½ pint/1¼ cups of water into a pan, add the sugar and heat until dissolved. Boil for 2 minutes. Break the cinnamon sticks in two and add them to the syrup, with the star anise. Remove the stalks and pits from the cherries and add them to the syrup. Bring the syrup to the boil, cover and leave to simmer for 2 minutes.

2 Lift the cherries out with a draining spoon and pack into two warm, dry, sterilized jars, with the spices. Boil the remaining sugar syrup rapidly for 5 minutes. Pour into the jars to half fill. Top up with the brandy.

Bramble Jelly

This jelly is best made with hand-picked wild blackberries. Make sure you include a few red, unripe berries for a good set.

INGREDIENTS

900g/2lb/8 cups
blackberries
300ml/½ pint/1¼ cups
water
juice of 1 lemon
about 900g/2lb/4 cups
caster (superfine)
sugar
hot buttered toast,
to serve

1 Put the fruit, water and lemon juice into a large saucepan. Cover the pan and cook for 15–30 minutes or until the blackberries are very soft.

2 Ladle into a large sieve lined with muslin (cheesecloth) and set over a large bowl. Leave to drip overnight to obtain the maximum amount of juice.

3 Discard the fruit pulp. Measure the exuded juice and allow 450g/1lb/2 cups sugar to every 600ml/1 pint/2½ cups juice. Place both in a large, heavy pan and bring the mixture slowly to the boil, stirring all the time until the sugar has dissolved.

4 Boil rapidly until the jelly registers 105°C/220°F on a sugar thermometer or test for setting by spooning a small amount on to a chilled saucer. Push the mixture with your finger; if wrinkles form on the surface, it is ready. Cool for 10 minutes.

5 Skim off any scum and pour the jelly into warm sterilized jars. Cover and seal while the jelly is still hot and label when the jars are cold.

Chutneys, Pickles & Mustard

Home-made chutneys and pickles, bursting with natural flavour, make marvellous gifts, so pack them in pretty jars, ready to take to friends, neighbours and hosts.

R ELISHES BRING SAVOURY dishes alive, adding a delicious tang to hot and cold meats, poultry, breads and cheeses. They are easy to make and the perfect way to deal with an excess of fruit or vegetables. Today, they are used as an accompaniment to succulent meats, but in the past they were a necessity, adding interest to salted meat – preserving meat by salting often ruined its flavour and texture. Interesting pickles, chutneys and mustards can still be used to transform a very plain meal into something special.

Pickling in vinegar is probably the easiest way to preserve vegetables. Use only stainless steel pans and clean wooden spoons. Never use pure metal lids, as the acid in the vinegar can react with it. Plastic-covered metal can be used, however. If you don't want to follow a particular recipe, buy pickling spice or ready spiced vinegar – the results will be less individual, but still very tasty.

Of Indian origin, traditional chutneys are a wonderful mixture of chopped fruits, spices, acids and sugar, usually slowly cooked until thickened.

ABOVE: Pickled shallots have a delicious sweet-sour flavour with none of the harshness of pickled onions. Put 675g/1½ lb shallots in a large heatproof bowl and soften them by pouring boiling water over them. Leave them to stand for 10 minutes, then peel them. Pack the shallots into large sterilized jars, adding a bay leaf to each jar. In a pan, heat 600ml/1 pint/2½ cups malt vinegar with 175g/6oz brown sugar, 50g/2oz salt and 10ml/2 tsp pickling spice. Stir continuously over a low heat until the sugar has completely dissolved, then bring the liquid to the boil. Remove the pan from the heat and add 7.5ml/1½ tsp balsamic vinegar for flavouring. Pour the liquid over the shallots to cover them completely. Add a circle of greaseproof (waxed) paper to the top of the jars, then seal with a screw-top lid. The shallots will be ready to eat in 2 weeks.

Apple & Ginger Chutney

Recipes for tangy chutney became very popular in Europe in the 19th century, when travellers to India brought them back. This chutney is a typical Indian recipe that has been passed down through the generations.

INGREDIENTS

1kg/2¼lb green apples	115g/4oz chopped
15g/½oz chopped	preserved stem ginger
garlic	450g/1lb seeded raisins
1litre/1¾ pints/4 cups	450g/1lb brown sugar
malt vinegar	2.5ml/½ tsp cayenne
450g/1lb chopped	pepper
dates	25g/1oz salt

1 Core and chop the apples, and chop the garlic. Place them in a large pan, and cover with the malt vinegar. Boil until soft.

2 Add the remaining ingredients to the pan and boil gently for 45 minutes. Spoon into sterilized jars, allow to cool and seal.

Garlic & Chilli Mustard

Delicious, aromatic home-made mustard matures to the most fragrant of relishes for eating with sausages, grilled steaks or boiled ham.

INGREDIENTS

40g/1½oz white	2.5ml/½ tsp ground
mustard seeds	turmeric
40g/1½oz black	1 dried red chilli
mustard seeds	1 large clove garlic
50g/2oz/¼ cup soft	200ml/7fl oz/scant
brown sugar	1 cup distilled
5ml/1 tsp salt	malt vinegar
5ml/1 tsp	10ml/2 tsp tomato
whole peppercorns	purée (paste)
a few cloves	

1 In a blender, blend the white and black mustard seeds, soft brown sugar, salt, peppercorns, cloves, turmeric, chilli and garlic. Gradually add the distilled malt vinegar to the dry ingredients a tablespoon at a time, blending well between each spoonful, then continue to blend until you have a coarse paste.

2 Blend in the tomato purée, then leave the mixture to stand for 10–15 minutes to allow the flavours to develop, before spooning it into warm sterilized small glass jars. Cover with greaseproof (waxed) paper discs, then seal each jar with a screw-top lid.

Jams & Jellies

Jams and jellies are the traditional way of using up the autumn fruit gluts. When jars are properly sealed and kept unopened their contents should last all through the year.

F RUITS THAT ARE JUST RIPE rather than fully ripe contain more natural pectin, a substance that helps jam to set. When using fruits that are naturally low in pectin, such as cherries, apricots and strawberries, setting can be helped by adding some high-pectin fruit such as apples, plums, quinces or blackcurrants. Alternatively, bought pectin can be added, or you can use a preserving sugar containing pectin. As well as producing consistent results, this simplifies the process, making it possible to produce jam within half an hour. To test for the setting point of jams and jellies, spoon a little of the mixture on to a chilled saucer. When the setting point has been reached, a skin will quickly form, which will wrinkle when pushed with your finger.

ABOVE: Tasty jellies and jams can be made from fruit we don't normally eat, such as bitter crab apples and quinces.

ABOVE: One of the mainstays of the traditional English breakfast, marmalade has a wonderful bitter-sweet flavour that's found in no other jam. The secret is in the rind, which is chopped up and cooked with the jam. Although marmalade can be made with any citrus fruit, the traditional recipe using bitter Seville (Temple) oranges is still the best. Wash and quarter 1kg/2¼ lb Seville oranges and 1 unwaxed lemon. Remove the flesh, pips and pulp, tie in a piece of muslin (cheesecloth) and place in a preserving pan. Slice the peel and add to the pan together with 2.2 litres/4 pints/9 cups water. Bring to the boil and simmer for 1½–2 hours until the peel is tender. Warm 1.75kg/4lb preserving sugar in the oven. Stir into the fruit until it dissolves, then boil rapidly to the setting point. Stand for 15 minutes. Pour into warm sterilized jars and seal.

Rosehip & Apple Jelly

A delicious tea-time treat made from windfall apples and rosehips gathered from the hedgerows, this jelly is rich in flavour and vitamin C. It makes a tasty safeguard against winter colds.

INGREDIENTS

1kg/2¼lb apples   450g/1lb firm ripe

preserving sugar   rosehips

1 Peel, trim and quarter the apples. Place them in a preserving pan, cover them with water and add 300ml/ ½ pint/1¼ cups extra water. Bring to the boil and cook until the apples are pulpy.

2 Coarsely chop the rosehips in a food processor, then add to the apples and allow to simmer for 10 minutes. Leave to stand for 10 minutes. Strain the mixture overnight through a thick jelly bag.

3 Measure the juice and allow 400g/14oz sugar for each 600ml/1 pint/2½ cups liquid. Warm the sugar in the oven. Bring the juice to the boil and stir in the sugar until it has dissolved, then boil until the setting point is reached. Pour the jelly into warm sterilized jars and seal.

Dried Apricot Jam

This is a wonderful jam that can be quickly made at any time of year using dried apricots and chopped almonds, both typical storecupboard ingredients.

INGREDIENTS

675g/1½lb dried   675g/1½lb preserving

apricots   sugar

900ml/1½ pints/   50g/2oz blanched

3¾cups apple juice,   almonds, coarsely

made with concentrate   chopped

juice and grated rind of

2 unwaxed lemons

1 Soak the apricots overnight in the apple juice. Pour both into a preserving pan and add the lemon juice and rind. Bring the mixture to the boil, lower the heat and leave to simmer for 15–20 minutes until the apricots are soft.

2 Warm the sugar in the oven and add to the apricots. Bring to the boil, stirring until the sugar has dissolved. Boil until the setting point is reached. Stir in the chopped almonds and leave to stand for 15 minutes before bottling in warm sterilized jars and sealing.

Teas, Tisanes & Herbal Drinks

Freshly brewed herbal teas make a delicious, healthy alternative to traditional tea. Herbal cordials have beneficial effects, too, and are very popular.

DELICIOUS AND REFRESHING, herbal drinks are soothing and have a restorative quality. Some, such as fruit cordial, are high in vitamin C, so can help to ward off winter colds, while others can relieve ailments such as anxiety, indigestion, headaches, sleeplessness, tension and depression. Herbal teas can be made with fresh or dried herbs; you'll need to allow twice as much fresh as dried material. Rosemary, mint and lemon balm, also known as melissa, are wonderful used fresh, while lemon verbena and chamomile are good used dry.

Herbs are potent, so don't exceed the recommended quantities given for ingredients, or drink more than a stated dose. Avoid herbal teas during the first 3 months of pregnancy, and don't give herbal teas to children under four.

ABOVE: Fresh peppermint helps digestion and makes an ideal ingredient for a refreshing cup of tea after a meal.

ABOVE & LEFT: The fragrance of lemon verbena is irresistible. Make a pot, using a few fresh leaves or 1 tsp/5ml of dried per cup of boiling water. Strain the hot liquid. Add a little honey for extra flavour and sweetness.

Elderflower Cordial

The sweetly floral flavour of this refreshing summer drink is a favourite with adults and children alike. It's perfect to serve as a non-alcoholic 'special' drink on celebration days. From a health point of view, it is also a great safeguard against colds, as elderflowers are anti-catarrhal and limes are rich in vitamin C.

INGREDIENTS

10 fresh elderflower heads	5ml/1 tsp citric acid
2–3 limes, sliced	5ml/1 tsp cream of tartar
675g/1½lb/3 cups sugar	1 litre/1¼ pints/ 4 cups boiling water

1 Wash and pick over the elderflowers and put them into a large bowl with the sliced limes, sugar, citric acid and cream of tartar. Leave to stand for 2 hours.

2 Pour in the boiling water and leave to stand for 24 hours. Strain into sterilized bottles and seal. The cordial will keep in the refrigerator for 2–3 months.

3 To serve, dilute with about twice as much chilled still or sparkling water.

RIGHT: Ease nerves with a tea made from a blend of 1 tsp each of dried lemon balm, chamomile flowers and peppermint in 600ml/1 pint/2½ cups boiling water. Allow to steep for 10 minutes and drink up to three times a day for no longer than 2 weeks.

ABOVE: A butterfly blend is a helpful tonic for the nervous system. It can help to relieve anxiety and depression and is also reputed to improve sexual function.

Make a blend of equal parts of dried St John's wort, porridge oats and damiana. Use 2 tsp of the mixture to 600ml/ 1 pint/2½ cups of boiling water and allow to steep for 10 minutes. Strain the boiled liquid. You can drink a cup of this tea up to three times a day, but cease drinking it after 2 weeks.

Index

apples, 52, 53, 56

bags, drawstring, 31
bathroom products, 38–43
bath salts, 43
beer stains, 13
body lotion, 41
body scrubs, 40, 41
bottling, preserves, 53, 56
breath-fresheners, 39
bruise ointment, 47
buttons, sewing on, 32

calendula cream, 46
candelabra, 21
candles, floating, 21
candlesticks, 21
cherries, cinnamon-spiced, 57
china and porcelain, 14–15
chutneys, 52, 58, 59
cold remedies, 48, 49
cordial, elderflower, 63
cosmetics, 44–5
cough remedies, 49
cutlery, 20, 21

decanters, washing, 16
dinner services, 15
dishwashers, china in, 14
drinks, herbal, 52, 62, 63
dusting powder, 45

earthenware, 15

face masks, 45
flowers and foliage, 34–5
fruits, 52, 53
    preserved, 53, 56–7
furniture, care, 7, 18–19

gargles, 48
garlic, medicinal use, 49
glassware: care of, 10, 16, 17
    frosting, 17

hand creams, 47
hangers, padded, 27
healing treatments, 38–9, 46–7
heat marks, on wood, 7, 18
herbs: for the bath, 43
    culinary, 52
    for drinks, 52, 62, 63
    in oils and vinegars, 54, 55
    remedies, 48–9

ironing, 25, 31

jams and jellies, 57, 60–1

lace, cleaning, 31
laundry, 24, 28–9, 31
lavender, 19
    "bottles", 27
    and clothes/linens, 25, 26
    essential oil, 44
    scent, 34
    and skin care, 44, 45, 46
linens: bed, 25
    recycling, 30–1
    storage, 25
    table, 12–13
lip balms, 46

marmalade, 60
medicinal remedies, 48–9
moisturizers, lavender, 45
moths, 25
motif patches, 33
mustards, 6, 59

napkin pockets, 17
napkins, 12, 13

oil(s): bath, 42, 43
    essential, 40, 42, 44
    flavoured, 52, 54, 55
    massage, 41

perfumed closets, 26–7
pickles, 52, 53, 58
plates, warming, 14
polish, wood, 18, 19
pot-pourri, 35
preserves, 52

scenters, 35
    drawer, 24, 25
sewing kits, 24, 32
sewing and mending, 32–3
sewing kits, 24, 32
shallots, pickled, 58
skin care, 44–7
soaps, hand-made, 40
stain removal, 12, 13, 24, 28, 29
steam facials, 44

teas, 52, 62, 63
tooth powder, 38

vaporizers, 35
vapour rubs, 47
vinegars, flavoured, 54, 55

washing, laundry see laundry
water marks, on wood, 18
wax stains, 13
wine stains, 13
wooden furniture, care, 18–19

Acknowledgements

Thanks to the following
photographers, project makers,
home economists and stylists:

Penny Boylan, Paul Bricknell,
Kathy Brown, Lisa Brown, Anna
Crutchley, Stephanie
Donaldson, Nicki Dowey, Tessa
Evelegh, Lucinda Ganderton,
Michelle Garrett, Juliana Goad,
Judith Gussin, Jessica Houdret,
Tim Imrie, William Lingwood,
Gilly Love, Maggie Mayhew,
Gloria Nicol, Debbie Patterson,
Spike Powell, Graham Rae,
Andrea Spencer, Isabel Stanley,
Lucinda Symons, Stewart and
Sally Walton, Jenny Watson,
Kate Whiteman, Steven Wooster
and Polly Wreford.